GET-INTO-IT

T0015062

GET INTO CHESS

RACHEL STUCKEY

CRABTREE
Publishing Company
www.crabtreebooks.com

Author: Rachel Stuckey

Editors:
Marcia Abramson, Philip Gebhardt, Janine Deschenes

Photo research: Melissa McClellan

Editorial director: Kathy Middleton

Proofreader: Wendy Scavuzzo

Cover/Interior Design: T.J. Choleva

**Production coordinator and
  Prepress technician:** Samara Parent

Print coordinator: Katherine Berti

Consultant: Artiom Samsonkin - Expert consultant,
International master, National Youth Coach.

Developed and produced for Crabtree Publishing
by BlueApple*Works* Inc.

Photographs

Shutterstock.com: © yanugkelid (cover background); © Karen
Struthers (cover boy left); © Pabkov (cover top left inset); © bitt24
(cover top right inset); Nerthuz (cover bottom right inset); © A_Lesik
(title page, p. 14 left, back cover left inset); © xtock (TOC); © Werner
Muenzker (p. 4 left); © katatonia82 (p. 5 right); © Will Thomass (p. 6);

© Sam Taylor (cover boy middle and girl right, p. 8 bottom, 9 bottom,
10 bottom, 11 bottom,
12 bottom, 13 bottom, 17 bottom, 19 bottom, 20 bottom, 22 bottom, 24
bottom, 25 bottom, 27 bottom, back cover top);

Creative Commons: Finlay McWalter (p. 4 right); © 2007, S.M.S.I., Inc. -
Owen Williams, The Kasparov Agency (p. 5 left);

Library and Archives Canada Cataloguing in Publication

Stuckey, Rachel, author
          Get into chess / Rachel Stuckey.

(Get-into-it guides)
Includes index.
Issued in print and electronic formats.
ISBN 978-0-7787-2639-5 (hardback).--ISBN 978-0-7787-2645-6
(paperback).--ISBN 978-1-4271-1790-8 (html)

1. Chess--Juvenile literature.   I. Title.

GV1446.S78 2016   j794.1   C2016-903387-2
                                        C2016-903388-0

Library of Congress Cataloging-in-Publication Data

Crabtree Publishing Company

www.crabtreebooks.com   1-800-387-7650

Printed in Canada/072016/EF20160630

Published in Canada
Crabtree Publishing
616 Welland Ave.
St. Catharines, Ontario
L2M 5V6

Published in the United States
Crabtree Publishing
PMB 59051
350 Fifth Avenue, 59th Floor
New York, New York 10118

Published in the United Kingdom
Crabtree Publishing
Maritime House
Basin Road North, Hove
BN41 1WR

Published in Australia
Crabtree Publishing
3 Charles Street
Coburg North
VIC, 3058

CONTENTS

WORLD'S FAVORITE MIND-CHALLENGING GAME

Chess is the world's most popular board game. It's also the world's oldest board game that is still played today. Most people agree that chess was invented about 1,500 years ago in India. Chaturanga is an Indian military strategy game with pieces that move on a board that is divided into squares. The game was introduced to the royalty of Persia in the 7th century and soon after in Arabia.

As the new religion of Islam spread throughout the world, the game followed. The **Moors** introduced chess to Spain starting in the 10th century. As the game spread through Europe, players changed the style of the pieces and the way they move. By the 15th century, the game had its modern form. There are also strategy games played in China that are similar to chess, such as xiangqi. But historians believe the game probably spread from India to China, and from China to India.

DID YOU KNOW?

Staying in Shape

Early chess pieces were detailed carvings of soldiers, elephants, and horses. The new religion of Islam banned images of humans or animals in art, so chess pieces became more abstract. The early European chess sets were based on the game played in the Islamic world, with the pieces taking on more European identities such as bishop and queen. The official chess set used today was designed in 1849 and named for chess master Howard Staunton. It combined the simpler abstract style of chess in Islamic countries, the European figures, and the artistic style of the day.

A group of 12th-century chess pieces called the Lewis chessmen was found in 1831 on the Isle of Lewis in the Outer Hebrides, in Scotland. The pieces represent one of the rare surviving medieval chess sets. The top row shows king, queen, and bishop. The bottom row shows knight, rook, and pawn.

CHAMPION CHESS

Today the top chess players in the world participate in international tournaments that lead to the World Chess Championship—the highest prize in chess. The championship is organized by the World Chess Federation or FIDE, from the French name Fédération Internationale des Échecs. The first World Chess Champion was Wilhelm Steinitz. Both men and women can be champions and there is no age requirement. There is also a Women's World Chess Championship, a World Youth Chess Championship for boys and girls under 18, and a Junior World Chess Championship for players under 20.

Hou Yifan of China (left) won her fourth FIDE Women's World Championship in March 2016 by defeating Mariya Muzychuk of Ukraine, the 2015 champion. The prizes included money, a trophy, a crown, a gold medal, and flowers. The match was played in Potocki Palace in Lviv, Ukraine.

CHALLENGING COMPUTERS

The best chess player in the world is a computer. **IBM**'s Deep Blue was the first chess-playing computer and took more than 10 years to develop. In 1996, Deep Blue won a game of chess against World Champion Garry Kasparov. But Kasparov won three games and tied two, winning the match 4 to 2. Then IBM made some adjustments. In their 1997 rematch, Deep Blue beat Kasparov by one game. Today, a computer will beat the best human player every time. But the chess game on your computer is designed to play at different skill levels and is programmed to play like a human!

Great chess players often excel at an early age. Garry Kasparov, who was born in 1963 in Russia, was well on his way to becoming a champion at age 11 (above). He held the top ranking in world chess from 1986 until he retired in 2005.

Chess is played on a square board made of 64 squares in rows of 8. The squares along each row alternate in color from white to black or light to dark. Each player has 16 pieces: 1 king, 1 queen, 2 bishops, 2 knights, 2 rooks, and 8 pawns. One player's pieces are white or a light color, and the other player's pieces are black or a dark color. The board must be set so that a white or light square is in the lower right-hand corner.

Players take turns moving their pieces according to the rules, and try to capture their opponent's pieces. The object of the game is to trap your opponent's king, so he can't escape. This is called checkmate.

CHESS PIECES AND CHESSBOARD LAYOUT

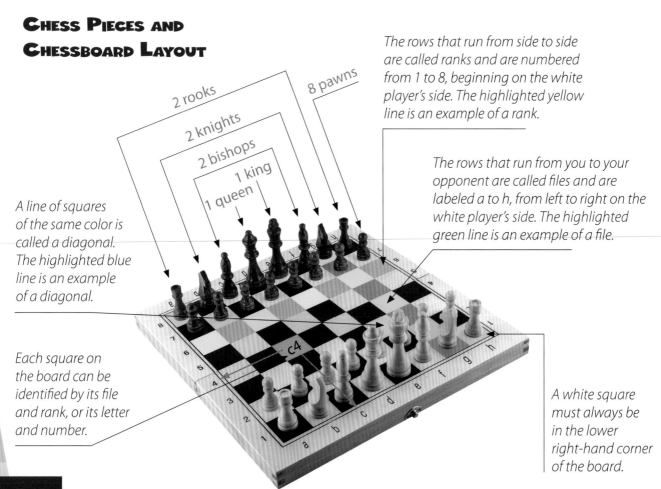

2 rooks

2 knights

2 bishops

1 king

1 queen

8 pawns

The rows that run from side to side are called ranks and are numbered from 1 to 8, beginning on the white player's side. The highlighted yellow line is an example of a rank.

The rows that run from you to your opponent are called files and are labeled a to h, from left to right on the white player's side. The highlighted green line is an example of a file.

A line of squares of the same color is called a diagonal. The highlighted blue line is an example of a diagonal.

Each square on the board can be identified by its file and rank, or its letter and number.

A white square must always be in the lower right-hand corner of the board.

c4

RECORDING CHESS GAMES

Entire games of chess can be recorded on paper using **chess notation**. The notation uses K for king, Q for queen, R for rook, B for bishop, and N for knight. Each move is recorded with the initial of the piece and the file and rank of the square it moves to, such as Ra5, or Qh4, or Bc6. (Ra5 means that the rook moved from where it was to square a5.) Pawn moves are recorded with just the square notation. (For example, c4 means the pawn moved from where it was to square c4.) You record a capture with an x. In official games and matches, chess players record each move they make. Chess players use these records to study their own games and the games of the chess masters.

NOTATION SYMBOLS AND LETTERS

Pawns have no notation letter because they are so many of them. It is easier to record them by their position on the board.

R

The notation letter for a rook is R.

N

The notation letter for a knight is N.

B

The notation letter for a bishop is B.

Q

The notation letter for a queen is Q.

K

The notation letter for a king is K.

RECORDING MOVES

Once chess pieces leave their starting position, their movements are registered using the letter and number combination grid.

This diagram shows a board three moves into the game recorded as

1. e4   Nf6
2. d3   Nxe4
3. dxe4

The diagrams below show details of individual moves that led to the recording above.

Move 1. white e4   black Nf6

Move 2. white d3   black Nxe4

Move 3. white dxe4

The d in front of xe4 specifies from which file the pawn did his capture.

Test Your Chess Skills! Page 28

THE ROOK

The rook looks like the tower of a castle or fort. It is the second most valuable piece on the board—more valuable than knights and bishops, but not as valuable as the queen. Together the rook and queen are known as major pieces. The rook is the easiest piece to understand and move.

What's in a Name?

In early versions of chess, the rook was actually a **chariot** *or carriage. The name "rook" likely comes from a Persian word for chariot, "rukh." After the game traveled to Spain and the rest of Europe, the chariot became a castle tower.*

The rook is worth 5 points. Each player starts with two rooks, one on each corner of the board.

White a1 and h1
Black a8 and h8

Test Your
Chess Skills!
Page 28

MOVING ROOKS

The rook moves in straight lines either along a rank or a file. Players can move their rooks as many unoccupied squares as they choose to. Rooks cannot jump over other pieces, but they can move to a square occupied by an opponent's piece and capture that piece. In a special move called **castling**, a rook can jump over its own king.

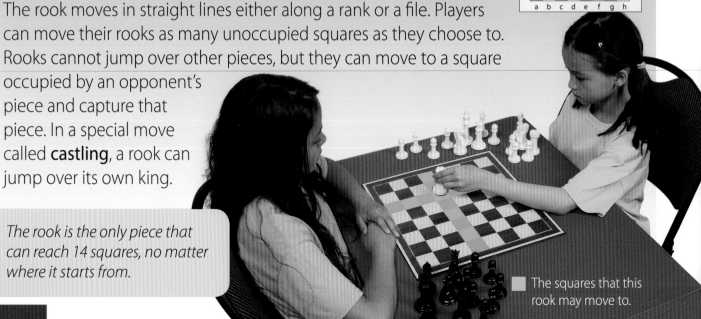

The rook is the only piece that can reach 14 squares, no matter where it starts from.

The squares that this rook may move to.

THE BISHOP

The bishop has a pointed top that is divided by a groove. The bishop is weaker than the queen and the rooks. Together with the knights, bishops are considered minor pieces. Like the rook, the bishop is easy to understand and move.

The bishop is worth 3 points. Each player starts with two bishops that begin the game two squares in from the rooks.

White c1 and f1
Black c8 and f8

MOVING BISHOPS

The bishop moves along diagonal lines in any direction. Players can move their bishops as many vacant squares as they choose to. Bishops cannot jump over other pieces, but they can move to a square occupied by an opponent's piece and capture that piece.

What's in a Name?

The bishop got its English name because it resembles the miter or hat worn by bishops. But in other languages, the piece has different names. In French and Romanian, it is named for the court jester. In German, Dutch, and Finnish, it is known as the "runner" or "messenger." In other languages, it is the hunter, the archer, or the officer. The piece was originally an elephant, and is still called that in Arabic and Russian. No matter what the piece is called, it looks and moves the same way.

Test Your Chess Skills! Page 28

The squares that this bishop may move to.

Bishops may be called light-squared or dark-squared because they always stay on the same color. The two white bishops will always be on different-colored squares. The two black bishops will also always be on different-colored squares.

9

THE QUEEN

The queen is topped with a crown with points all the way around. The queen is the most powerful piece on the board. It is almost twice as valuable as a rook. Together with the rooks, the queen is a major piece. The queen can move like a rook and a bishop.

The queen is worth 9 points. Each player starts with one queen that begins the game on its own color on the d file.

White d1
Black d8

MOVING QUEENS

The queen can move in straight lines, along either ranks or files, and along diagonal lines in any direction. The queen has many options! Players can move their queen as many vacant squares as they choose. But like bishops and rooks, the queen cannot jump over other pieces. The queen can move to a square occupied by an opponent's piece and capture that piece. Because it is so valuable and powerful, most players protect their queen at the beginning of the game.

Can a Queen Rule?

In early versions of chess, the queen piece was actually a **vizier** *or adviser to the king called the firzan or firz. In Russian, the piece is still called ferz. In early European chess games, the piece became known as the queen. Some historians believe it was the popularity of queens such as Eleanor of Aquitaine, Isabella of Spain, and Elizabeth I that influenced the change. It was the Spanish game that gave the queen its power, around the same time that Queen Isabella united Spain into a great empire.*

Test Your Chess Skills! Page 28

Queens can move in eight different directions. They are so important that players who lose their queen early in a chess game very likely will lose the game, too.

The squares that this queen may move to.

THE KNIGHT

The knight is shaped like the head of a horse. The knight is weaker than the queen and the rooks. Together with the bishops, knights are considered minor pieces. But the knight has a special power—it is the only piece on the board that can jump over other pieces.

The knight is worth 3 points. Each player starts with two knights that begin the game one square in from the edge.

White b1 and g1
Black b8 and g8

Test Your Chess Skills! Page 28

MOVING KNIGHTS

The knight moves in an L pattern. It moves two spaces in any direction, then one space to the side. The L pattern does not need to be open squares. Players can jump their knights over their own pieces, or over their opponent's pieces. And a knight can capture an opponent's piece on its landing square.

Special Skills

The knight is the only piece a player can move before moving at least one pawn. Because of this, the knight plays an important role in chess openings. And knights can come into play earlier than queens and bishops. Knights are most useful close to the action in the center of the board. The knight piece has always been able to jump. In the early Indian version of the game, the knight was a soldier on horseback or one of the cavalry and could jump over the opponent's pieces.

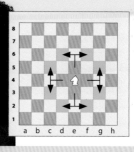

Knights need room to execute their L-shape moves, so players try to position them away from the rim of the chess board.

The squares that this knight may move to.

THE PAWN

The pawns are the smallest pieces on the board. They have rounded tops. They are relatively weak, and they are often sacrificed to allow for future moves of other pieces. Pawns cannot move very far, but they do have special moves that give them more power.

What's in a Name?

*English uses the word "pawn" to identify a person who is easily manipulated or **sacrificed**. This meaning comes from chess. The word pawn is probably from a Latin word for foot soldier. In German, pawns are called bauers or farmers, and in Spanish they are peones or laborers.*

White a2 to h2
Black a7 to h7

The pawn is worth 1 point. Each player starts with eight pawns that begin along the second rank, in front of the other pieces. Pawns are often named for the piece behind them at the beginning of the game.

MOVING PAWNS

The pawn can only move one space forward into open squares—it can never move backward or to the side. If a pawn is still on its original square, it can move forward by two squares. Pawns capture an opponent's piece by moving on a diagonal. Pawns are the only piece that can move differently to capture. When a pawn reaches the opponent's first rank, it gets a **pawn promotion** and takes on the qualities of any other piece, except a king and a pawn. Usually, players choose to promote their pawn to a queen.

Test Your Chess Skills! Page 28

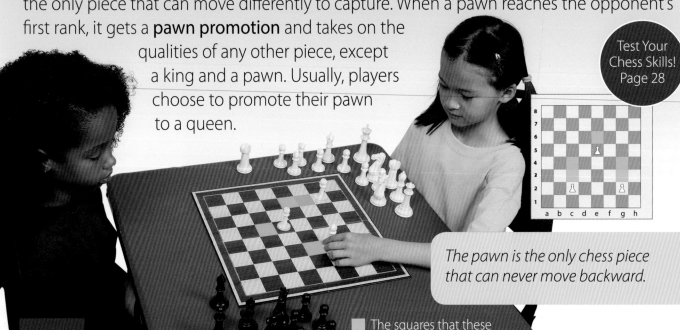

The pawn is the only chess piece that can never move backward.

The squares that these pawns may move to.

THE KING

The king is topped with a crown that has a small cross rising in the middle. The king is the tallest piece on the board and the most valuable. But it is also the weakest piece. Because the main purpose of the game is to checkmate your opponent's king, the king must be protected at all costs.

The king has no point value because it cannot be taken like other pieces. Each player starts with one king that begins in the center of the rank on the opposite color, next to the queen.

White e1
Black e8

MOVING KINGS

Like the queen, the king can move in any direction along a rank, a file, or a diagonal. However, the king can only move one square at a time. The king may capture an opponent's piece. If the king and a rook have not yet been moved, and the knight and bishop are not between them, a player may **castle** the king.

The King's Weakness

*European history is full of warrior kings who fought in battle. And when a king died, his **heir** would take the throne and continue to defend the kingdom. So why is the king so weak in chess? In the original Indian version of chess, the king was an **emperor**. An emperor in India was a wise leader who had devoted generals that fought the battles. In the ancient worlds of India and Persia, when an emperor was captured or killed, the empire fell.*

Test Your Chess Skills! Page 28

Kings are not allowed to make moves that would put them in danger of being captured immediately.

The squares that the king may move to.

MOVE YOUR PIECES SMARTLY

The most basic rules of chess involve how the pieces move. White always makes the first move. Players draw to determine who will play white. You may not touch a piece unless you plan to move it—you cannot stop a move and start again. This is called touch move and in "friendly" games such as we are encouraging here, the players agree in advance whether they are playing touch move. You must move a piece on your turn—you cannot pass. Moving your pieces from their starting position is called **developing**.

Each player has their own clock or timer—your timer is paused during your opponent's turn, and your opponent's timer is paused when it is your turn.

CHESS CLOCK

Chess was played without time limits until the 19th century. Both players and spectators complained about the slow pace, so the chess clock was invented. This device consists of two adjacent clocks with buttons to stop one clock while starting the other. Different levels of play set their own rules for how much time to allow.

| Pawn | Knight | Bishop | Rook | Queen | King |

WHAT'S THE POINT?

While chess pieces have a numerical value, players are not awarded any points in chess. The purpose of the value is to help predict the winner—a player with more valuable pieces or points on the board has the advantage. The points value also helps players make decisions about how to play. It may not be worth attacking a 3-point knight if it means losing a 5-point rook. A sacrifice involves losing a piece on purpose so you can gain a tactical advantage or an advantage of position.

Moving Out

In the first stage of a game, only the pawns, bishops, and knights should move forward to secure a good position in the center of the board. Queens and rooks stay protected in reserve to be used later in the game.

The Minor Pieces and Pawns

Bishops and knights are the minor pieces. Players use them to gain position before bringing in the major hitters. Pawns join them in the initial moves and help to control the board in the opening stage.

Bishop   Knight

The Major Pieces

Queens and rooks are the major pieces. Players try to keep them protected early in the game, and save their power for later stages in the game.

Queen   Rook

Special Rule – Capturing a Pawn En Passant

Pawns move forward one square, except on their first move, when they can move two squares. However, if your pawn moves two squares to avoid being captured, your opponent can still capture your pawn. On the next move, your opponent can move their pawn to the square your pawn would have occupied if it had only moved one square, and capture your pawn while it's passing. This is called capturing a pawn en passant.

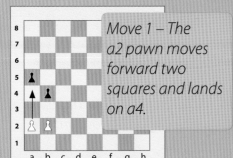

Move 1 – The a2 pawn moves forward two squares and lands on a4.

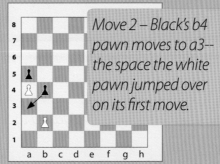

Move 2 – Black's b4 pawn moves to a3-- the space the white pawn jumped over on its first move.

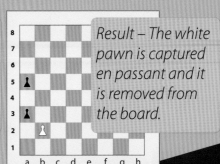

Result – The white pawn is captured en passant and it is removed from the board.

THE OPENING

The opening is the beginning of a game of chess. It goes from the very first move until players have developed their major and minor pieces. What happens in the opening can influence the entire game. The aim of the opening is to build a strong position on the board. You should not be concerned about capturing your opponent's pieces—instead you should concentrate on moving your pieces into strategic positions. For hundreds of years, chess players have studied the different ways of opening a game. Many chess openings are named—this makes it easier to talk about them.

FIVE OPENING TIPS

There are as many rules and tips for chess openings as there are chess masters, but these are five common tips.

1. Develop your minor pieces right away— the knights, bishops, and pawns.

Do not let your knights and bishops sit on the first rank—these pieces are only useful if they can move around the board.

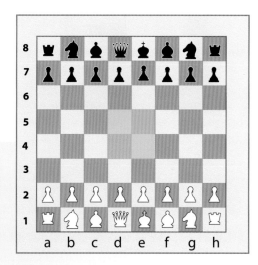

Opening moves generally focus on the four squares at the center of the chessboard—d4, e4, d5, and e5. The squares that touch on these four can also be important in chess strategy. Whoever controls the central squares will have better access to the whole board and an easier path to victory.

2. Do not move a piece twice before move 10.

If you waste time moving a knight back and forth, your opponent can develop more pieces and occupy better strategic positions on the board. There are times you need to move a piece twice to avoid being captured, to capture an opponent's piece, or to create a weakness in your opponent's position.

3. Castle your king before move 10.

Staying in the middle of the rank is dangerous for the king. Castling protects your king and develops your rook. Before castling, you must first move all the pieces between the king and the rook. The king and the rook cannot have moved first. Don't move the pawns that are in front of the castled king.

Test Your Chess Skills! Page 29

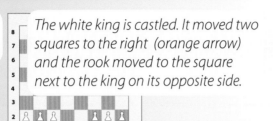

In this diagram, the white kings is not castled yet.

The white king is castled. It moved two squares to the right (orange arrow) and the rook moved to the square next to the king on its opposite side.

4. Do not bring out your queen too early.

The queen is the most powerful piece on the board. If the queen is developed too early, she may be captured by a minor piece. Instead, focus on the knights, bishops, and pawns first.

5. Develop your pieces toward the center of the board.

When your pieces are in the center of the board, you have more options to attack, capture, or block.

What Is Castling?

*Castling is both an offensive and defensive move. To castle, the king and the rook move together. Castling is the only time two pieces move at the same time in chess. However, to castle properly, the king has to move first. Always move your king first with one hand. Once the king has moved two squares to right or to the left depending which way you castle, you can then move the rook over the king (this is called jumping over the kings head) and land it right beside the king. A king in **check** cannot castle, and it cannot pass through check either.*

Once you learn to apply the five basic tips for opening, you can build on them to advance your game. Don't make moves too quickly. Think carefully about each move before you make it.

OPENING TACTICS

Chess players study and practice openings to ensure a strong start in every game. A mistake made in the opening can determine the outcome of the game. Openings have names such as the Giuoco Piano, the French Defense, the Caro-Kann Defense, and the Queen's **Gambit**. Each opening has different variations and defenses depending on each player's second and third moves. Both players must be prepared to play many different opening variations and defenses, depending on how their opponent moves in response.

Test Your Chess Skills! Page 29

OPEN VS CLOSED

Pawn structure, or the placement of the pawns, determines whether a game is open or closed. In a closed game, the pawns are spread out through the middle, blocking other pieces from moving easily. Knights are useful in closed games because they can jump over the pawns. In an open game, the ranks, files, and diagonals are clear. Bishops are more useful in open games because they can move long distances on the diagonals.

Open Game

Closed Game

An open game set up shows a lot of free space in the middle of the board that allows the pieces to move around freely.

In a closed game set up, the middle of the board is occupied by many pieces which makes further moves more challenging.

King's Gambit

Moves
1. e4   e5
2. f4
The next natural move is
2. ...   exf4

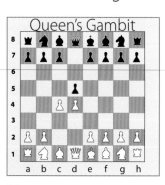
Queen's Gambit

Moves
1. d4   d5
2. c4
Black can accept the gambit with
2. ...   dxc4
or decline the gambit and play
2. ...   e6

OLD ROYAL GAMBITS

The King's Gambit begins with moves e4 and e5. White then moves the f4, pawn. The Queen's Gambit is similar, but starts with moves d4 and d5 followed by c4. In the Queen's Gambit, the d4, pawn is protected by the queen. Because of this difference, the Queen's Gambit is more popular in master level play. Both openings have been in use since the 1500s.

THE SICILIAN DEFENSE

The Sicilian Defense begins after white opens with e4 and black responds with c5. There are many variations of the Sicilian Defense, depending on white's second move. Statistically, black is more likely to win with a Sicilian Defense than by following white's move with e5. World Chess Champions Bobby Fischer and Garry Kaparov made the Sicilian Defense very popular.

Sicilian Defense

Moves—1. e4   c5

The Sicilian Defense is named for Sicily, a Mediterranean island that is part of Italy. Starting in the 1500s, this tactic spread from Italy and now is used by players at all levels of the game.

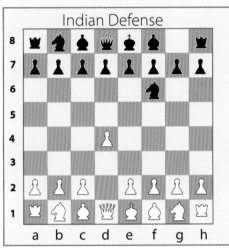

Indian Defense

Moves—1. d4   Nf6

Indian Defenses start with white's d4 move followed by black's Nf6 move. The Indian Defense is a risky opening, where black purposely gives up the center of the board.

INDIAN DEFENSES

In Indian Defenses, black uses an **asymmetrical** response to white playing the d4, pawn. Instead of responding with d5, black plays Nf6, developing a knight on the first move. The Indian Defenses were named for Mahesh Banerjee, a great Indian chess player in the 1850s who favored this style of opening.

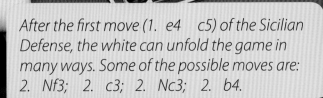

Players use the Sicilian Defense to control the key d4 square. It is the most popular and successful counter to white's e4 opening.

After the first move (1. e4   c5) of the Sicilian Defense, the white can unfold the game in many ways. Some of the possible moves are: 2. Nf3; 2. c3; 2. Nc3; 2. b4.

THE MIDDLEGAME

The opening moves and the endgame may be more dramatic, but the middlegame is where many chess games are decided. The middlegame generally begins once each player has developed their pieces and protected their king. But there is no fixed point where the opening ends and the middlegame begins. Here are some general strategies that will help you play a strong middlegame.

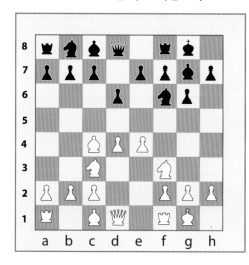

This middlegame position was played by Bobby Fischer, a chess prodigy and world champion from the United States who died in 2008. Notice how white has taken control of the center.

CONTROL OF THE CENTER

The most important battles happen in the center of the board, so the player that controls the center has the advantage. Controlling the center is not the same as occupying the center. Control of the center means that a player has developed their pieces in a way that allows them to attack the four squares in the center of the board (d4, d5, e4, e5). For example, a player might move their knights and bishops into positions toward the sides, which allows them to attack their opponent's pieces near the center.

The hard work of establishing a good opening pays off in the middlegame. The player who controls the center spaces will be able to attack and defend more easily.

TAKING INITIATIVE

When a player makes a move that threatens their opponent, it forces the opponent to respond with a defensive move. This prevents the opponent from launching their own attack. The player who makes threats that cannot be ignored has the **initiative**. The strongest example of a threat that cannot be ignored is putting the king in check.

Test Your Chess Skills! Page 29

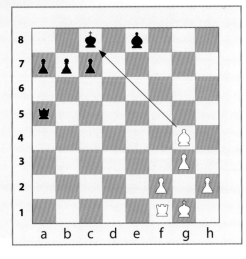

In the middlegame, players plan moves to put the enemy king in check, or under direct attack. This diagram shows the black king in check by the white bishop.

THE EXCHANGE

The goal of the middlegame is to capture your opponent's pieces. In an even match, your opponent will capture many of your pieces, too. When both players capture pieces one right after the other, it is called an exchange. First, one of the players captures an opponent's piece. When the opponent captures a piece on the next move, it is called a recapture. When the pieces are equal in value, such as bishops or knights, it is called an even exchange. If the values of the captured pieces are not equal, it is an uneven exchange. Then the player who captures the higher-value piece wins the exchange. Because the player with more valuable pieces on the board has an advantage, understanding the exchange tactics is important in the game of chess.

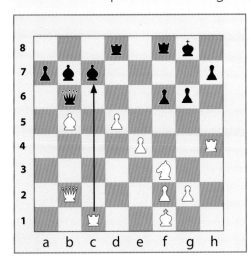

A minor piece (a bishop) is being exchanged for a major piece (a rook) in the diagram at left. Winning the rook wins the exchange.

ATTACK TACTICS

WEAKENING YOUR ENEMY

Checkmate usually can't be achieved in just a few moves. To get there, each player tries to weaken the opponent by establishing a superior position in the center of the board, then capturing enemy pieces. Players must be on the lookout for spots where the enemy has grown weaker, while making sure their own pieces are safe. It may take dozens of such middlegame moves to get to the endgame.

MIDDLEGAME TACTICS

In the middlegame, players execute their strategy in a series of planned moves. To make these moves, pieces must be kept active, which means they are not locked into one spot on the board. When the opponent leaves pieces open, an active piece is ready to attack. Some of the popular attacking tactics are the fork, the pin, and the skewer.

THE FORK

The fork is a classic chess move. When you move a piece into a position where it threatens two of your opponent's pieces, you have created a fork. With two threats, your opponent must protect the most valuable piece, which allows you to capture the other piece under threat on your next move. There are many ways to create a fork. Although any chess piece can be used to create a fork, knights and pawns are good in this situation. Pawn forks often mean you have to sacrifice a pawn, but you still win the exchange.

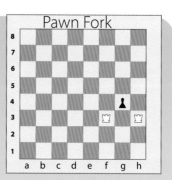

Knight Fork   Pawn Fork

In a knight fork (above left), the white knight has seized the opportunity to fork the king and queen. Black will have to escape the check by moving the king, which frees white to capture the queen. Two major pieces are under attack, but only one can escape.

Test Your Chess Skills! Page 29

Knights can execute forks without risking capture because of their unique L-shaped move.

The Long-Range Pieces
Queens, rooks, and bishops are called long-range pieces because of the way they can roam over the board. They are the only pieces that can make pins and skewers.

Test Your Chess Skills! Page 29

THE PIN

The pin is a move that traps a lower-value piece, such as a pawn or knight, in front of a higher-value piece such as the queen or the king. When a piece is pinned, it cannot move without exposing the higher-value piece. You must use a rook, bishop, or queen to pin your opponent because these pieces move in straight lines. If you let a knight or pawn sit on the same rank, file, or diagonal as the king, the knight or pawn may become pinned.

Absolute Pin

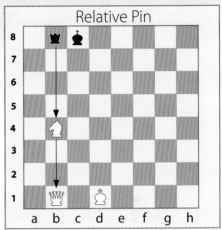

A pin is absolute when there is no legal way a piece can escape the attack. At left, the knight on d8 is absolutely pinned.

A pin is relative when the piece under attack can be moved legally, but doing so will expose another piece to danger. Usually that piece is higher-ranking, as in the diagram at right.

Relative Pin

This is a relative pin because if the white knight moves, the black rook captures the white queen.

Test Your Chess Skills! Page 29

THE SKEWER

The skewer is the opposite of the pin. In the skewer, you threaten a high-value piece. By forcing that piece to avoid capture by moving, you expose the piece it was protecting. Like the pin, the skewer can only be performed with a rook, bishop, or queen. The skewer often involves the king. When the king is in check, it must move. This may expose the queen or a rook.

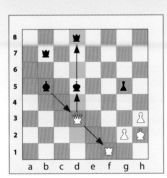

A skewer is absolute when it involves a king that must move to get out of check. In a relative skewer, the threatened piece does not have to be moved.

The diagram above shows the difference between an absolute skewer and a relative skewer. The green line shows the black king in an absolute skewer by the white queen. The black king must move out of check, but then the black rook will be lost. Now follow the orange line to see a relative skewer. The white queen can move to safety, but the white rook will be captured on the next move. If the rook moves, the queen will fall. There is a choice with a relative skewer – even if it's not a happy one!

DEFENSE TACTICS

To win a game of chess, you must capture your opponent's pieces. But you must also defend your pieces with every move. Think about the consequences of each move—do this by looking at each of your opponent's possible moves. You must also defend the ranks, files, and diagonals to prevent your opponent from moving their rooks, bishops, and queen long distances. Remember the value of the pieces—your rooks and queen are almost as important as your king.

THE ENDGAME

Just like with the opening and middlegame, it is difficult to say when the middlegame ends and the endgame begins. But the endgame usually begins when there are very few pieces on the board and the king can be used as an attacking piece. With fewer pieces on the board, the king can be used to attack your opponent, as there are fewer risks of checkmate.

Like the opening, the endgame is studied and practiced. Endgames are organized into different categories, based on the pieces that remain. For example, there are king and pawn endings, queen and pawn endings, bishop versus knight endings, or queen versus two rooks endings, just to name a few! Endgame strategy can revolve around trying to promote a pawn. A new queen can prove to be decisive.

After you learn about different endgame positions, try setting them up on the board and practicing with friends.

CHESS PUZZLES

The best way to practice the endgame is to complete chess puzzles. Chess puzzles were once a common feature of newspapers and chess magazines. These puzzles were often based on famous chess games, and the real outcomes were published in the next issue. Today, chess enthusiasts can find puzzles online to practice endgame patterns.

THE DRAW

Sometimes there is no way for either player to win. When this happens, the game ends in a tie, which is called a draw. Players can agree to a draw at any time. Two very common situations that cause a draw are a **stalemate** and **perpetual check**.

A stalemate happens when one player's king is not in check, but the player has no legal moves with the king and even with other pieces if he has any left. (Remember, you cannot move your king into check).

In perpetual check, one player continually puts their opponent in check, but cannot achieve checkmate.

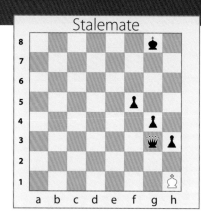

This game has resulted in a stalemate. The white king is not in check, but it has no square to move to without being put in check.

Insufficient Material

Chess games also end in a draw when neither player has enough pieces left to checkmate the enemy king. This is called insufficient material and occurs only when the remaining pieces are:

- King and bishop against king
- King and two knights against king
- King and one knight against king
- Only the two kings

Some games end with no winner or loser, which is a draw. Win, lose, or draw, players still shake hands.

RESIGNING

A player may resign, or give up the game to their opponent. This happens at the highest level of chess, when players can see several moves ahead and know what the outcome will be. Sometimes players will signal that they have resigned by tipping over their king. But usually players simply say "I resign," and shake their opponents' hand.

ENDING THE GAME

CHECK

Whenever one of your opponent's pieces is in a position to take your king on the next move, your king is in check. When no move will save your king, it is checkmate and the game is over.

DISCOVERED CHECK

A powerful way to surprise an opponent is by giving a discovered check. This happens when a player's piece blocks one of his or her own pieces from giving a check to the opponent's king. The blocking piece moves out of the way and check is "discovered" on the board.

GETTING OUT OF CHECK

There are three ways of getting out of check.

- Move your king.
- Block the checking piece.
- Capture the checking piece.

If none of these three options exist, it is checkmate.

Test Your Chess Skills! Page 29

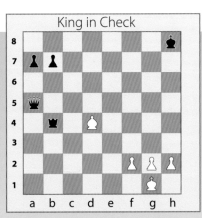

The white bishop has the black king in check.

The king is out of check.

Now the black queen has moved to block the check...

... and the black rook can capture the white bishop.

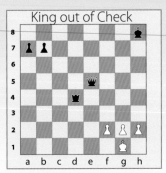

After the black rook makes its capture, the king is safely out of check.

CHECKMATE

To achieve checkmate, you need to put your opponent's king in check and block the three ways of getting out of check. The king may be blocked from moving to a safe square by his own pieces that are being used to protect the king. This situation is called **smothered mate**.

CHECKMATE STRATEGIES

Checkmate strategies usually involve two attacking pieces. One piece puts the king in check. The second piece blocks the king's escape. Because the king can only move one square, the key to checkmate is to control the squares around the king. The best pieces for giving checkmate are the queen and rooks.

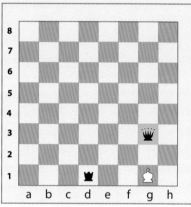

For example, the rook can put the king in check on the rank, and the queen can prevent the king's escape on the file or diagonals.

While the king is the most important piece on the board, the queen is the most versatile. The queen can move in eight different directions, which makes it the best piece for checkmates.

After learning opening moves, and middlegame and endgame tactics, it's time to master checkmate skills.

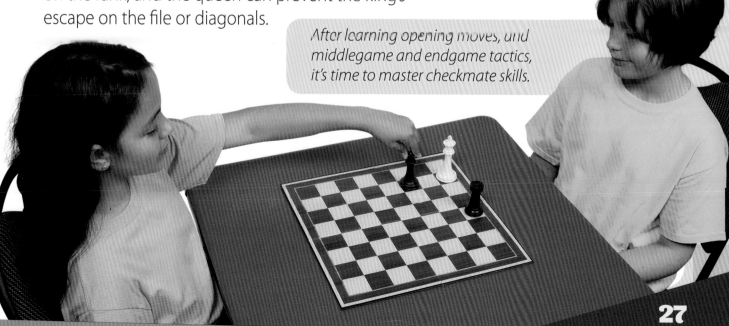

TEST YOUR CHESS SKILLS

Test your newly learned chess skills using the exercises on this spread.
Find the correct answers on Page 32.

RECORD THIS GAME

Move 1. white   black

Move 2. white   black

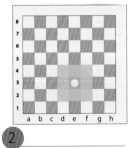

Move 3. white   black   Move 4. white

Record the moves below

Move 1. _____

Move 2. _____

Move 3. _____

Move 4. _____

PLACE PIECES ACCORDING TO THE NOTATION (Mark with arrows)

Moves
1. e4 e5
2. Nf3 Nc6

Moves
1. Nf3 Nf6
2. c4 b6

Moves
1. b4 e5
2. Bb2 Nc6

RECOGNIZE THE PIECES BASED ON THEIR MOVES

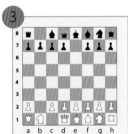
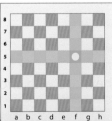

1 _____ 2 _____ 3 _____ 4 _____

Each chess piece has a particular way of moving across the board. It is important to be familiar with the options. Name the piece based on the moves highlighted in the diagrams and write your answers in the space provided. Check pages 8 to13 for correct answers.

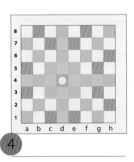

5 _____ 6 _____

THE OPENING

RECOGNIZE THE OPENING

A. _____ game

B. _____ game

The diagrams above show two different approaches to a chess game opening stage. Based on what you know about handling the open space in the middle of the board, which diagram represents the open, and which represents the closed game.

CASTLING

Can you castle a king in this situation? Think about reasons why you could, or why you could not.

The king is safely castled. Which part of the move came first—the move shown by the orange arrow, or by the black arrow?

THE MIDDLEGAME

EXCHANGE EXERCISE

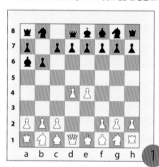

In the diagram above, the white bishop is being exchanged for the black bishop. Mark the exchange with an arrow.

FORK EXERCISE

How many forks can you see in the diagram above? Mark them with arrows.

PIN EXERCISE

Can you recognize a pin in the diagram above? Mark the pin with an arrow.

SKEWER EXERCISE

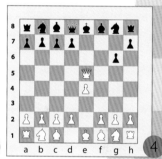

Can you recognize a skewer in the diagram above? Mark the skewer with arrows.

THE ENDGAME – UNDERSTANDING CHECK

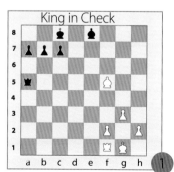

King in Check

Which piece has the king in check in the diagram above? Mark the move with arrow.

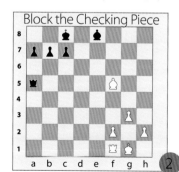

Block the Checking Piece

According to the move patterns of chess pieces, which piece can block the checking piece, is it Ra5, c7, or Be8. Mark your choice with arrow.

Capture the Checking Piece

According to the move patterns of chess pieces, which piece can capture the checking piece, is it Ra5, Be8, or c7. Mark your choice with arrow.

29

LEARNING MORE

BOOKS

Kids' Book of Chess by Harvey Kidder and Kimberly Bulcken Root,
New York: Workman Publishing, 1990.

Checkmate! My First Chess Book
by Garry Kasparov, London: Gloucester Publishers, 2004.

Learn Chess Quick by Brian Byfield and Alan Orpin, London: Batsford, 2010.

Chess for Kids by Michael Basman, New York: DK Children, 2006.

WEBSITES

ChessKid
www.chesskids.com
ChessKid is a part of Chess.com and offers lessons and a library of resources for new players and support for clubs and school teams. Kids 12 and under can sign up to play chess online against other kids around the world. Players 13 and up can sign up to play on Chess.com.

US Chess
new.uschess.org
The US Chess Federation or US Chess represents the United States in the World Chess Federation (FIDE) and organizes the US Chess Olympiad Team. Visit this website to learn more about tournament play and rankings in the United States.

Chess Federation of Canada
www.chess.ca
The Chess Federation of Canada represents Canada in the World Chess Federation (FIDE). Visit this website to learn more about tournament play and rankings in Canada.

Chess Corner
www.chesscorner.com
Chess Corner is a website created by chess enthusiasts. The site offers free tutorials, online games, and information about chess.

Learning Chess
learningchess.net
This site offers some free online lessons for beginners, as well as some paid lessons for more advanced players.

GLOSSARY

asymmetrical Having two sides or halves that are not the same

castle Special move where the king moves two squares to the side and the rook jumps over the king, it must be the first move for both the king and rook

chariot A two-wheeled cart pulled by a horse, and used for races and military operations in the ancient world

check Under direct threat of capture on their opponent's next turn

chess notation A system for recording chess moves which allows you to replay your own games, as well as games of other players to learn their strategies and tactics

developing The moving of pieces from their starting position to new positions where their activity can be increased

emperor Someone that rules an empire

gambit A move at the beginning of a game that involves sacrificing a piece, usually a pawn, with the hope of achieving an advantage

heir Someone who will inherit another person's wealth or title when that person dies

IBM One of the first computer companies in the world, formerly called the International Business Machine Corporation

initiative The action of going on the attack or applying pressure to your opponent

Moors A Muslim culture from North Africa that ruled Spain and Portugal from the 8th century to the 15th century

pawn promotion When a pawn reaches the opposite side of the board, it can be changed into a different piece, such as a queen

pawn structure The placement of pawns on the board during the game

perpetual check When a player puts their opponent's king in check on every move, without being able to create a checkmate

sacrifice When a player voluntarily offers a piece in exchange for a favorable advantage

smothered mate Checkmate by a knight in which the king's escape is blocked by his own pieces

stalemate When a player whose turn it is has no legal move, but his king is not in check

vizier Historical term for the emperor's adviser in Muslim empires

INDEX

TEST YOUR CHESS SKILLS ANSWERS

Record This Game Exercise Answers

Move 1. _____ e4   g6 _____
Move 2. _____ d4   Bg7 _____
Move 3. _____ Nc3   d6 _____
Move 4. _____ Bc4 _____

Recognize the Pieces Based On Their Moves Answers

1. bishop   4. queen
2. king   5. pawn
3. knight   6. rook

Recognize the Opening Answers

A. Open Game   2. Closed Game

Castling Answers

1. No, you have to move all the pieces between the king and the rook before castling.
2. The move shown by the orange arrow came first. To castle, the king has to move first, followed by the rook's move.

Place Pieces According to the Notation Answers

The Middlegame Exercises Answers

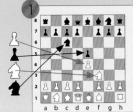
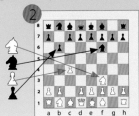
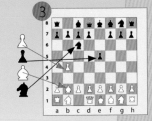
Exchange · Fork · Pin · Skewer

The Endgame Exercises Answers

King in Check — The white bishop (Bf5) has the black king (Kc8) in check.

Block the Checking Piece — Be8 can make the Bd7 move along the diagonal and block the checking Bf5.

Capture the Checking Piece — Ra5 can make the RxBf5 move along the file and capture the checking Bf5.